IMAGES
*of America*

# Lost Amusement Parks of Kentuckiana

**ON THE COVER:** Attracting attention from its opening in 1892, the waterfront area of Shawnee Park was annexed by the city in 1895 with the surrounding land for further land development. Here, bathers at Shawnee Beach enjoy swimming in the Ohio River near the clubhouse at Fontaine Ferry Park in the 1930s. (Courtesy of Gary Matheis.)

IMAGES
*of America*

# LOST AMUSEMENT PARKS OF KENTUCKIANA

Carrie Cooke Ketterman

Carrie Cooke Ketterman

ISBN 978-1-4671-2830-8

Published by Arcadia Publishing
Charleston, South Carolina

Printed in the United States of America

Library of Congress Control Number: 2017951938

For all general information, please contact Arcadia Publishing:
Telephone 843-853-2070
Fax 843-853-0044
E-mail sales@arcadiapublishing.com
For customer service and orders:
Toll-Free 1-888-313-2665

Visit us on the Internet at www.arcadiapublishing.com

*To my parents, who inspired the desire to preserve local history, and to Jeff for your never-ending support of my next big idea.*

# Contents

# ACKNOWLEDGMENTS

From an early age, I have always had an incredible interest in amusement parks from days gone by. Many a family summer vacation was spent roaming the old boardwalks of Coney Island in Brooklyn, New York. Fascinated by the charm and history, I began looking for amusement parks in my own backyard. Not being alive during the heyday of such wonderful local parks, numerous libraries, local archives, and individuals are to thank for their many hours of work in preserving this local history. Without their hard work and dedication, this book would not have been possible nor would future generations discover and appreciate these long-lost parks. The New Albany Floyd County Public Library, specifically Kaitlyn Tisdale of the Stuart B. Wrege Indiana Room, and Allison Frederickson of the Jeffersonville Township Public Library offered a treasure trove of information and photographs about the Glenwood Park and Rose Island history, respectively. A very special thank-you to Gary Matheis, son of Bill Matheis, who was the owner of Kiddieland and assistant manager to Jack Singhiser of Fontaine Ferry Park, for the very generous use of your Fontaine Ferry family photo album and for all the fascinating stories of Fontaine Ferry and Kiddieland. These very rarely seen photographs of Fontaine Ferry will provide wonderful memories for people who remember attending this local treasure. Special thanks to David Barksdale, John Findling, Andy Albatys, Jason Rayburn, Scott Allen, Barbara Montgomery, Johnny Urbanavage, and the Louisville District, US Army Corps of Engineers for use of your amazing postcards and images that preserve this local history. Thank you also to Steve Wiser for being the connection to this wealth of knowledge about the history in our community. Thank you to Charlestown State Park, and especially Jeremy Beavin, for the use of photographs and wealth of information on the walking tours of Rose Island. All the images in this book are credited to the gracious individuals and libraries that provided them. There are so many lovely images at the New Albany Floyd County Public Library and the Jeffersonville Township Public Library that unfortunately could not make it into the book due to quality, but I encourage readers to visit these libraries and see these historic images in person. There is also a wealth of knowledge and images on social media groups that provided many wonderful details and the history behind the images. Thank you to Tessa Wilkinson for your expertise and support. I also wish to thank my editor at Arcadia Publishing, Caitrin Cunningham, for your guidance and assistance with this project. Lastly, thank you to my parents, Jon and Diane, for inspiring me to preserve history and for encouragement during this project, and to my husband, Jeff, for your support and love not just on this project but in everything.

# INTRODUCTION

Following the success of Coney Island in New York in the 1880s and the 1893 World's Columbian Exposition in Chicago, hundreds of amusement parks began to spring up all over America. These picnic and amusement destinations, first called pleasure gardens, appeared as early as the 1550s in England and proved to be so good for business that the parks flourished and became even more elaborate. The banks of the Ohio River, where picnic grounds were quite popular and steamer travel was abundant, provided an ideal location for amusement parks to thrive in the Kentuckiana area.

In early America, these amusement parks took the form of picnic grounds. The grounds provided open space away from the dirt and grime of booming cities and featured concerts, sometimes bathing, and always food. Not only did these parks provide entertainment for guests, they also promoted business for local transportation companies like the steamer *America*, which took visitors to Rose Island. Many transportation companies saw an opportunity to promote their own business. The New Albany Traction Company purchased the Glenwood Park area from the well-known Beharrel family of New Albany for its new destination park. The *Idlewild*, now *Belle of Louisville*, was refitted to become an excursion steamer that took people to Fontaine Ferry and Rose Island.

The 1893 Chicago World's Columbian Exhibition provided the initial model that inspired most, if not all, American amusement parks. It introduced a new idea of combining rides, shows, and concessions, separated in its own contained area that we now call a midway. These expositions attracted massive crowds seeking entertainment, education, recreation, and trade. The man who is largely recognized as the creator of the amusement park is to George C. Tilyou. He was a masterful entrepreneur who first created the concept that has become known as the amusement park.

The history of the amusement park cannot be told without mentioning Coney Island in Brooklyn. This five-mile stretch of beach provided a pleasant and mostly undeveloped area that vacationers could visit for close and cheap recreation away from the bustling city. As the industrial landscape grew, and the cities became overrun with soot and smoke, people began to look for areas outside the city that provided a body of water with plenty of fresh air. Coney Island became the first amusement park to offer featured attractions like the famous Steeplechase racetracks and the first amusement railroad in 1884 by Lamarcus Thompson called the Switchback Railroad. Tilyou, who is credited with being the first to own an array of single rides that created a midway, built his more than 125-foot version of a Ferris wheel he had seen at the 1893 Chicago fair and inspired a new wave of feature attractions at various parks. Early amusement parks like Coney Island paved the way for future parks, and people flocked to these early amusement areas for their attractions, rides, and entertainment. As more parks were created, they grew more elaborate and lavish to entice visitors.

The amusement parks that popped up along both sides of the Ohio River near Louisville, Kentucky, and the southern Indiana area of Charlestown and New Albany saw a wealth of visitors and economic success for transportation companies and businessmen alike. Chronologically, Fern Grove first welcomed guests to its picnic grounds as early as 1885 and was later purchased in 1923 by David Rose, a Louisville businessman who renamed the park Rose Island. Fern Grove was initially purchased by the Louisville and Jeffersonville Ferry Company for picnic grounds. Rose took the land, a peninsula at the mouth of Fourteen Mile Creek about three miles south of Charlestown, and started calling it an island. By calling the park Rose Island, Rose attracted a new crowd of anxious visitors excited to explore this new exotic "island" modernized with its own electrical power plant, ice plant, running water, hotel, dance pavilion, skating rink, summer cottages, dining hall, and an Olympic-sized swimming pool.

Also on the Indiana side of the Ohio River, Glenwood Park opened to visitors on July 1, 1903, and welcomed thousands of attendees daily. At the turn of the 20th century, New Albany's street railway system inaugurated the interurban system of electric cars connecting New Albany, Jeffersonville, and Louisville. The renamed Louisville & Southern Indiana Traction Company provided easy and steady transportation from these three locations and dropped visitors directly at Glenwood Park. These 12 acres of land were the perfect place for visitors to spend a summer day. There was something for everyone at Glenwood Park, with an open-air theater, a stage that could seat 1,200 people, a dance pavilion, a bandstand, rides, a shooting gallery, boating in the nearby creek, bathing complete with swimsuits to rent, a bowling alley, a miniature railroad, swings, an athletic field, and a refreshment stand.

Across the river in an area now known as Chickasaw Park sat White City. Promoted as the Coney Island of the South, White City first opened in 1907 but struggled against another local amusement park, Fontaine Ferry. Several White City amusement parks appeared throughout the country, the most successful being in Chicago, Denver, and Cleveland. The White City location in Louisville was the first to offer a water roller coaster attraction called Shoot the Chutes, in which riders were plunged into a large lagoon while sitting in a wooden coaster seat. The competition with the already successful Fontaine Ferry along with a massive fire on the property in 1910 caused White City to close in 1912. It was later sold for residential development.

The most iconic and successful park in the Kentuckiana area was Fontaine Ferry Park, which was in operation from 1905 to 1969. Fontaine Ferry was located at 230 South Western Parkway, at the western end of Market Street, on 64 acres of land in western Louisville near the Ohio River. Fontaine Ferry Park was the largest park in the area in terms of entertainment. It offered a variety of 50 rides and attractions, a swimming pool, skating rink, and theater. The dark side of Fontaine Ferry and ultimate reason for its demise was a result of the park being segregated until 1964. Post segregation, the park only continued to operate for an additional five years before undergoing a few name changes, including Ghost Town on the River in 1972 and then River Glen Park in 1975, in an attempt to reopen, but these were not successful. Today, Fontaine Ferry is a residential area and part of Shawnee Park in West Louisville.

Following the success of Fontaine Ferry, Kiddieland, a much smaller amusement park located on the east side of Seventh Street and Berry Boulevard in Shively, across from Arlan's Department Store, operated during the 1950s and 1960s. Being focused primarily on young adventure seekers, Kiddieland offered rides like a miniature train, carousel, fire truck ride, miniature airplane and boat rides, and pony rides.

# *One*

# Life along the Ohio

Recreation in Louisville and the southern Indiana area along the Ohio River has always revolved around the river itself. The Kentuckiana area was discovered only because while traveling along the Ohio, explorers encountered a major natural navigational barrier, the Falls of the Ohio. Louisville, Jeffersonville, and New Albany's ideal location situated along the Falls of the Ohio destined them to become intertwined with the steamboat industry. Through steamboats and river travel, people, freight, ideas, and news traveled faster, and the region was linked to national networks of commerce, communication, migration, and popular culture. During the peak years, New Albany was second only to Pittsburgh in steamboat production and became Indiana's largest town by 1850. In 1860, Louisville was ranked 12th among the nation's cities. (Author's collection.)

During the 1880s, swimming had become a popular recreational pastime across the country. Louisville's first public swimming pool was not built until 1915, so many living in the area chose the natural swimming area of the Ohio River. During the 1890s, swimming beaches became very popular along the shores of the Ohio. Beaches reached from the west end of Louisville all the way east of the Kentucky & Indiana Railroad bridge. (Author's collection.)

Built in 1914, the *Idlewild* first operated as a passenger ferry between Memphis, Tennessee, and West Memphis, Arkansas. She hauled cargo such as cotton, lumber, and grain. Upon coming to Louisville in 1931, the *Idlewild* began making regular excursion trips between Fontaine Ferry Park and Rose Island. (Author's collection.)

With the Falls of the Ohio creating a natural barrier, the cities of Louisville, New Albany, and Jeffersonville were founded along the banks of the Ohio River. Being near the Ohio, these cities were booming with riverboat traffic. Steam navigation was not introduced to the area until Robert Fulton guided the *New Orleans* through the waters, and public excursions were offered during the weekend upon its docking in Louisville. The earliest known steam ferry service began around 1827. (Author's collection.)

The waterfront of Shawnee Park in West Louisville opened in 1892. The city annexed the park along with the surrounding land, prompting the installation of streetcar lines out to the more scenic grounds overlooking the Ohio River. (Author's collection.)

In 1798, Capt. Aaron Fontaine of Virginia settled in Louisville and established a flatbed ferry service on his riverbank farm. With the increased river traffic, entrepreneurs like Tony Landenwich realized an opportunity. Landenwich purchased Captain Fontaine's Ohio River estate and began to build a hotel resort, restaurant, and bicycle track. This image shows a crowd of people outside the bathing house along Shawnee Beach, the land settled by Fontaine and now owned by Landenwich. (Courtesy of Gary Matheis.)

As cities grew, so did means of transportation. The Kentucky & Indiana Terminal Railroad (K&I) operated 130 miles of track, and by 1886, the company had constructed an Ohio River bridge. K&I eventually operated a steam commuter train service, the Daisy Line, named after its yellow cars running from downtown Louisville across the bridge to New Albany. (Author's collection.)

The *Idlewild*, built in 1914 and renamed the *Avalon* in 1947 and the *Belle of Louisville* in 1962, docks along the Ohio River to let visitors onboard after a long day at Fontaine Ferry Park. (Courtesy of Gary Matheis.)

Visitors arriving by steamboat would dock at a small Market Street beach along the Ohio River. The sloping hills of Fontaine Ferry Beach were framed by large trees and provided a picturesque swimming spot on hot summer days. (Courtesy of Gary Matheis.)

Fontaine Ferry Park's 64 acres were located at 230 Southwestern Parkway, at the western end of Market Street. There was a road that led down to the river in the area, called Fontaine Ferry Road. However, many mispronounced it and called it Fountain Ferry. There is a local map from 1855 that lists the name as Fountain Ferry Road. Not wanting to miss out on any business, the last owner, Jack Singhiser, advertised using both names. (Author's collection.)

FERN GROVE, ON THE OHIO RIVER

One of the most popular pleasure resorts in the Kentuckiana area was found at Fern Grove on the Indiana side of the Ohio River. The Louisville and Jeffersonville Ferry Company made regular excursions for visitors to enjoy the beautiful picnic grounds surrounded by nature. (Author's collection.)

# *Two*

# Fern Grove and Rose Island

Surrounded by water from Fourteen Mile Creek and the Ohio River, one and a half hours by boat from the foot of Fourth Street, sat Fern Grove. An ideal picnic ground dating to the 1880s, Fern Grove served as a delightfully cool spot to spend a pleasant afternoon. Steamboats on the Ohio River historically were used for cargo, but with the introduction of railroads and the profits associated with getting people to destinations faster, steamers saw the opportunity to offer their services for excursions. Fern Grove first opened as a picnic ground for church groups, and the River Excursion Company brought them by steamboat. The natural beauty of the grounds was very enticing and an ideal location for a picnic. The land offered a sweeping view of the Ohio River, stunning lookouts with lush hills, woods called Lover's Lane, and the dominating feature known as Devil's Backbone, a rocky crag rising several hundred feet above the river. (Author's collection.)

ROSE

In this 1926 photograph, visitors to Rose Island depart the steamer *America*, which has just docked. An early account of a visitor to Rose Island states that the river entrance to Rose Island was one of its most attractive features. Here, visitors caught their first glimpse of the beauty of the island. A wide concrete walk extended from the landing to the native stone gates with large iron Gothic lampposts. A large electric sign was visible at night for miles up and down the river. From the main entrance, well-lit gravel walkways branched out in all directions. (Courtesy of Charlestown State Park.)

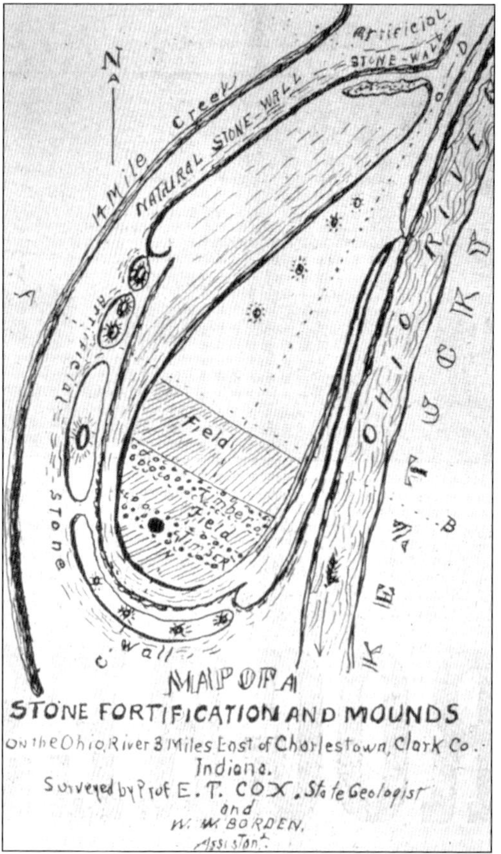


Journalist Joe Creason observed that the area known as Rose Island is in reality a peninsula-like strip of land with a steep, pear-shaped ridge that rises back from the Ohio River along the southern Indiana mainland. From the top of the ridge, 14 miles west, the skyline of downtown Louisville showed as fingers of brick and stone against the horizon. (Courtesy of Jeffersonville Township Public Library.)

The name Fern Grove came from the pioneers who floated down the Ohio River on flatboats and settled on the Indiana side, at Charlestown Landing. There was a flat area under a steep ridge full of ferns. (Courtesy of Jeffersonville Township Public Library.)

David B.G. Rose was originally from Nicholasville, Kentucky, and came to Louisville with only $20 to his name. He turned out to be a very successful businessman and owned the Standard Printing Company, whose clients included the *Courier Journal*. Unfortunately, the Great Depression caused the resort to take a financial hit. Rose Island continued to operate until January 1937, when a flood wiped out most of the park. In an effort to keep Rose Island operational, Rose eventually lost his wealth and was forced to rent a small spare bedroom in which to live. (Courtesy of Charlestown State Park.)

Crowds of onlookers stand on the banks of the Ohio River under the Rose Island sign watching fireworks on a summer evening. The Rose Island sign was an impressive feature during this time of no rural electricity. A generator on Rose Island provided the power to light up the sign. (Courtesy of Stuart B. Wrege Indiana History Room.)

Fern Grove was used as church picnic grounds when the area first opened. These were simple outings taken on riverboats with basket lunches. The *Sunshine* excursion boat would load at the foot of Fourth Street and took about two hours from the dock to landing at Rose Island. Visitors usually arrived by noon and could enjoy the forested area with lots of shady trees and picnic tables and benches for their picnic lunch. The steamers usually provided entertainment such as quartets or live music during the ride. (Courtesy of Jeffersonville Township Public Library.)

With the invention of automobiles, visitors traveled along a steep and winding road from Highway 62 down from the Indiana side and parked along Fourteen Mile Creek. After paying a quarter, they walked across the 400-foot swinging suspension bridge 50 feet above the creek to the park. Marvin Bernhart recalls, "I played on that swinging bridge constantly. My sister would get on there and I'd get that thing moving and bouncing, she'd get to screaming and my mother would give me heck." (Courtesy of Charlestown State Park.)

Once the use of automobiles as transportation was introduced to the area, Rose Island became quite the place to go on dates for an evening of dancing. There was a wooden ticket booth near the suspension bridge. Visitors arriving to Rose Island paid their entry fees here and then set off for a day of adventure at the park. If one drove by automobile, parking was free, but it was 25¢ to walk across the bridge that crossed Fourteen Mile Creek. (Courtesy of Charlestown State Park.)

This Indiana picnic ground was an immensely popular recreational area and was very successful for the river excursion companies. Rose Island was the perfect place for frolic and innocent fun. (Courtesy of Charlestown State Park.)

Rose Island was thought of as the ultimate summer resort, with 20 cottages rented out to those wishing to get some clean air away from the city. The cottages were very complete and compact. They consisted of a bedroom, a commodious living room, a bathroom, and a combination dining room and kitchen, and were fully furnished. The kitchens had kerosene ranges, a refrigerator, and other kitchen appliances. Each cottage had a front yard of about a hundred feet and a splendid view of the Ohio River from the front porch. (Courtesy of Jeffersonville Township Public Library.)

The picturesque peninsula of Fern Grove, featuring many acres of riverfront property, proved to increase the value of the new amusement park of Rose Island. The island became a summer resort and a holiday place for both private and public picnic parties. The grounds of the park were improved by adding paving stones so that in the event of a rainstorm, the water would drain off rapidly, insuring dry picnic grounds. (Courtesy of Charlestown State Park.)

During the early days of Fern Grove, the Fern Cliff Hotel sat at the entrance of the boat dock overlooking the Ohio River. This Victorian-style hotel served fine food morning, noon, and evening. It also hired many well-known orchestras to play dance music daily, even on Sundays. (Courtesy of Jeffersonville Township Public Library.)

David Rose made sure to provide plenty of provisions to accommodate large crowds visiting the island. Visitors could make arrangements to use the picnic grounds or spend the entire summer in one of the cottages. Rose Island was also modernized to provide an abundance of water for the restaurant, public toilets, cottages, and the park itself. (Courtesy of Charlestown State Park.)

For guests at the Rose Island resort, an evening in the dance hall was the perfect end to a summer day. While live music played, couples waltzed and tangoed across the dance floor. By the late 1920s and early 1930s, new dance crazes such as the Lindy Hop and the Charleston emerged. During the day, the dance hall doubled as a roller skating rink. It had an organist who would play music for the skaters. One of the favorite songs was the *Skater's Waltz*. Workers at the dance hall would clean the floor following skating and put dance wax on the floor for the dancers. (Courtesy of Charlestown State Park.)

A feature attraction of Rose Island was the swimming pool. It measured 110 feet by 42 feet and was reported to be the first filtered-water swimming pool in the Midwest. (Courtesy of Charlestown State Park.)

At a time when homes had no air-conditioning, a dip in Rose Island's swimming pool was the ultimate way to cool off on a hot summer day. Swimmers could climb onto a round platform in the pool's center and spin around and around, or use nearby trees as diving boards. The pool even provided a concession stand where visitors could rent a swimsuit for the day. (Courtesy of Jeffersonville Township Public Library.)

Thomas Lindley was a lifeguard from 1934 to 1937. He remembers the pool being built in 1934 and recalls it was "a dandy of a pool" for the time. He said his biggest problem was keeping people from climbing the trees and diving in. He was hired as the first lifeguard for the pool. Lindley was pleased with his wages of $5 a day, which was quite a bit of money to a teenager in those times. (Courtesy of Jeffersonville Township Public Library.)

*Spend Your Vacation At Home In Comfort*

*Boating, Swimming – Excellent Cuisine At Beautiful Rose Island*

DINING ROOM SERVICE MORNING, NOON AND EVENING, DAILY AND SUNDAY.

*Music for Dinner and Evening Dance by Rose Island Orchestra.*

AMPLE facilities for accommodating large crowds. Commodious cottages, complete with modern furnishings, present an atmosphere of home, while the natural beauties of the Island portray all of the great out-doors.

**Accessible to Motorists**

Take River Road to Prospect; thence straight ahead to Rose Lane; thence to Rose Island Ferry where free ferriage is available every ten minutes.

Those desiring to make reservation for large parties are requested to call Long Distance, Rose Island, Indiana, and ask for Mrs. Dix. For full particulars regarding rental of cottages telephone Main or City 3500.

ROSE ISLAND COMPANY
INCORPORATED
222 South First Street Louisville, Ky.

Steamer excursion advertisements showed the services offered by various companies. The steamer *America* was a side-wheeler of graceful proportions, with the most complete appointments of any river craft used exclusively for excursion purposes. Her numerous decks were kept spotlessly clean, with perfect ventilation throughout, giving the excursionist the benefit of the refreshing river breezes, both to and from the island. (Courtesy of Jeffersonville Township Public Library.)

According to Erskine Brook's column, "Civic Gossip," "For a decade this Indiana picnic ground has been the most popular of all picnic and recreational grounds around Louisville because of the river excursion it affords before reaching the place of frolic and innocent fun. The land was almost lost had Mr. David Rose not stepped in with his vision of Rose Island. The owners of the land were not interested in out of town businessmen and were looking for a local corporation to take over the property." (Courtesy of Stuart B. Wrege Indiana History Room.)

Although Rose Island offered amusement rides, most visitors flocked to the island for the basic pleasures it offered. Alice James remembers her experience visiting Rose Island as a child in the 1920s. She noted the purpose was to "go up there, sit out in the fresh air, and enjoy a picnic spot." She remembers the feeling of freedom to roam around. (Courtesy of Jeffersonville Township Public Library.)

The Rose Island Company could supply up to 100,000 gallons of water per day to the park. It was purified by the same method as the water supplied by the City of Louisville. The Rose Island Company said there was no superior water anywhere for drinking, cooking, or bathing. In addition, there were several mineral wells for those who desired water with supposed medicinal properties. Because there was no nearby town from which to secure ice, Rose Island had its own ice plant—a very substantial plant with the capacity of 10 tons per day, including refrigeration. It supplied not only the needs of the restaurant, grounds, and cottages, but it also sold surplus to neighbors for miles around. (Courtesy of Jeffersonville Township Public Library.)

This 1928 snapshot shows two children on pony rides at Rose Island. The park also included a pony track with as many as 15 Shetland ponies. For just 5¢, a child could take a pony ride. In addition to the ponies, Rose Island included a little zoo. Zoos and exotic animals were popular amusements in the early 20th century. The zoo at Rose Island included monkeys, wolves, and even alligators. The alligators were kept in a stone water fountain with a small moat. The best-known resident of this tiny zoo was a black bear named Teddy Roosevelt. (Courtesy of Jeffersonville Township Public Library.)

On August 17, 1932, the *City of Memphis*, a Louisville excursion steamer, sank in the Ohio River. All 781 passengers on board were saved, but the steamer was destroyed. In 1934, the *Idlewild* replaced the *City of Memphis* and is still in service today as the *Belle of Louisville*. (Courtesy of Louisville District, US Army Corps of Engineers.)

Men and women gather along the Ohio River in this early 1920s photograph. A trip to Rose Island also meant a chance to dress up in one's best clothes. Women wore dresses and men wore suits and hats. The summer cottages are just behind them through the trees. Behind the cottages was the Walkway of Rose, which featured stone columns on either side and iron arches stretched across the columns overhead. Electric lights were hung above the arches to illuminate the path. (Courtesy of Jeffersonville Township Public Library.)

David Rose thought of every detail when he created Rose Island. There was a Rose Island market menu in the dining hall, which included fresh eggs from the flock of 30 hens owned and cared for by the Rose Island Company. The restaurant on the grounds could seat 500 guests at one time under the covered pavilion. In addition to the outdoor dining room and the use of the dance hall, there was seating for 1,600 people. (Courtesy of Jeffersonville Township Public Library.)

The Rose Island Company owned a herd of Jersey cows and operated its own dairy for the benefit of the patrons of the Rose Island restaurant. There was milk, cream, and butter served at the restaurant. This was another instance where the Rose Island Company tried to go above and beyond expectations for visitors coming to its summer resort. (Courtesy of Jeffersonville Township Public Library.)

Lovie Decar, a Jefferson County resident, recalled an adventure to Rose Island. She wrote that the boat left the Madison landing at 8:00 a.m. Her mother was up at 4:00 a.m. the day of the trip, frying chicken and making potato salad for her picnic basket. When the boat arrived at Rose Island, they scrambled up to the park to get a picnic table. After enjoying a picnic lunch, they had all day to enjoy the amusements and activities. The departure whistle sounded at 4:30 p.m., and the boat departed for Madison at 5:00 p.m. People danced all the way home and were back at the Madison landing in time for a steamer to carry out a moonlight excursion to Carrolton and back. (Courtesy of Jeffersonville Township Public Library.)

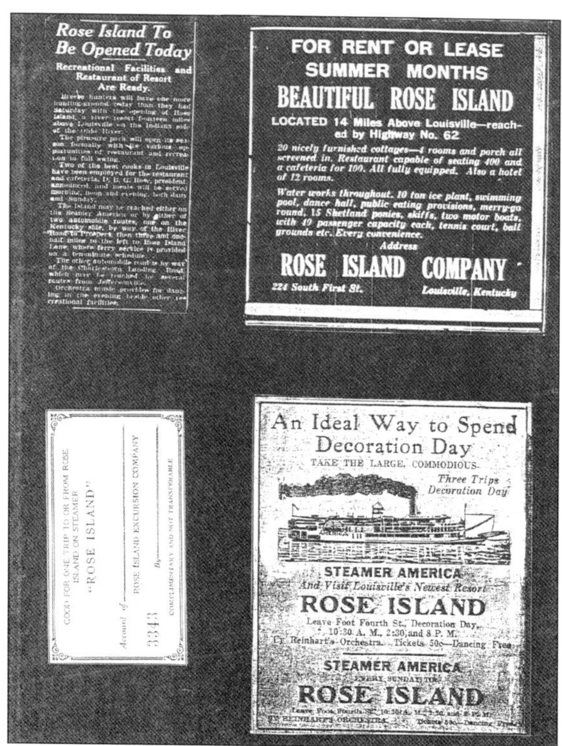

*Rose Island To Be Opened Today*

Recreational Facilities and Restaurant of Resort Are Ready.

FOR RENT OR LEASE
SUMMER MONTHS
BEAUTIFUL ROSE ISLAND
LOCATED 14 Miles Above Louisville—reached by Highway No. 62

*20 nicely furnished cottages—4 rooms and porch all screened in. Restaurant capable of seating 400 and a cafeteria for 100. All fully equipped. Also a hotel of 12 rooms.*

*Water works throughout. 10 ton ice plant, swimming pool, dance hall, public eating provisions, merry-go round, 15 Shetland ponies, skiffs, two motor boats, with 49 passenger capacity each, tennis court, ball grounds etc. Every convenience.*

*Address*

ROSE ISLAND COMPANY
*224 South First St.* *Louisville, Kentucky*

GOOD FOR ONE TRIP TO OR FROM ROSE ISLAND ON STEAMER
"ROSE ISLAND"
*Account of* ____
ROSE ISLAND EXCURSION COMPANY
3343 *By* ____
COMPLIMENTARY AND NOT TRANSFERABLE

An Ideal Way to Spend Decoration Day
TAKE THE LARGE, COMMODIOUS
*Three Trips Decoration Day*
STEAMER AMERICA
*And Visit Louisville's Newest Resort*
ROSE ISLAND
Leave Foot Fourth St., Decoration Day, 10:30 A. M., 2:30, and 8 P. M.
Cy Reinhart's Orchestra. Tickets 50c—Dancing Free

STEAMER AMERICA
EVERY SUNDAY TO
ROSE ISLAND

After visitors enjoyed a midday picnic lunch, there was more time to play before packing up and leaving around 4:00 p.m. The steamboat ride back to Louisville was shorter, thanks to the current, and often included a dance for the adults. There were chairs around the dance floor, and while the adults enjoyed their dancing and the music, most children would fall asleep. (Courtesy of Jeffersonville Township Public Library.)

The main entrance to Rose Island from the Ohio River featured three stone columns. Gates were later attached to these columns. There was an iron pipe on the top of the columns with an arching Rose Island sign. Each letter of the Rose Island sign was lit by big screw-in light bulbs. (Courtesy of Scott Allen.)

The giant electric Rose Island sign was also used as a navigation guide for boats. Fourteen Mile Creek was given its name because it is located 14 miles upstream from the Falls of the Ohio. River captains knew that once they passed Rose Island, there were only 14 miles until the boat came upon the Falls of the Ohio. (Courtesy of Jeffersonville Township Public Library.)

# *Three*

# Glenwood Park

Glenwood Park was situated between New Albany and Jeffersonville on Silver Creek. It offered all the amusements of a well-regulated park, including boating, bathing, fishing, baseball grounds, a dancing hall, and more. Many considered Glenwood the ideal park as it was thoroughly lit by electricity at night and had an abundance of shade during the day. Advertisements featuring the "Big Red Cars" announced special arrangements to take passengers from the Louisville Depot by the interurban via the Big Four Bridge and Jeffersonville. At the turn of the 20th century, New Albany's street railway system was purchased by the Insull brothers of Chicago. They inaugurated the electric interurban system connecting New Albany, Jeffersonville, and Louisville under the name of the Louisville & Southern Indiana Traction Company. It was the custom of the traction moguls in the nation to develop ideas to increase use of their systems, and in New Albany, the attraction became Glenwood Park—a resort where people could spend the lazy, hazy days of summer—which they reached by riding the interurban cars. (Author's collection.)

Canoe and boating parties were very popular. Many additional campers from Louisville, New Albany, and Jeffersonville came to Glenwood Park each week for a pleasant vacation on the banks of Silver Creek. (Courtesy of Stuart B. Wrege Indiana History Room.)

Glenwood Park opened on July 1, 1903, as Silver Creek Park with Gov. Winthrop Durbin as the guest of honor. It included flower gardens, a bandbox, picnic grounds, a Ferris wheel, pavilions, a baseball diamond, a tennis court, a miniature railroad, camping facilities, and lots of room for just relaxing throughout its 24 acres. The name was short-lived, as someone higher up than the stockholders of the traction company decided it would be Glenwood Park, which it remained from 1903 until its last day. (Courtesy of David Barksdale.)

There was a concrete dam on Silver Creek to permit canoeing and fishing. This dam is the only visible reminder of the park and can be seen today from the I-65 bridge on Spring Street. It is still a favorite fishing spot. (Courtesy of David Barksdale.)

Near the turn of the 20th century, an interurban line came through Jeffersonville from Louisville to New Albany. In those days, it was not uncommon for such lines to construct parks to attract more passengers and increase business. The Louisville & Southern Indiana Traction Company did not want to be outdone, so it decided to build a park where the tracks crossed Silver Creek, which is approximately where the old Spring Street Bridge is now. (Courtesy of David Barksdale.)

Silver Creek, Spring Street, and Beharrell Avenue bound the park, and the alley behind Glenwood Court was in two sections—Glenwood Park and Glenwood Athletic Field. The land was originally part of the Illinois or Clark Grant, given to one of George Rogers Clark's men, Levi Todd, by the Commonwealth of Virginia. Other owners from various times were Harvey Scribner and Benjamin Tuley, Ezekiel Day, and the Beharrell family, for whom the avenue was named. These were all prominent property owners of early New Albany. (Courtesy of Stuart B. Wrege Indiana History Room.)

The *New Albany Weekly Ledger* announced the arrival of the new bathing pier in 1919. Anderson G. Moore, booster and manager of Glenwood Park, had completed notable additions to the attractions at the park in the form of a large new bathing pier and high dive. Several hundred bathers could be seen there during the torrid days, finding relief in the cool waters of the creek. (Courtesy of Stuart B. Wrege Indiana History Room.)

Carpenters take a break from working on the Glenwood Park grandstand in the summer of 1905. (Courtesy of Stuart B. Wrege Indiana History Room.)

During the late 1800s and early 1900s, the people of New Albany spent many pleasant hours strolling the great grove of beech trees along the south bank of Silver Creek. There were a number of trails through here that came together at the dam and went upstream to an area known as "Indian Trail," so named because many Native American relics were found along the site. (Courtesy of Stuart B. Wrege Indiana History Room.)

A historical document from Bebe Cody of the Floyd County Historical Society notes that the Louisville & Southern Indiana Traction Company never owned the Glenwood Park Athletic Field. The 10 acres were leased from Nora Duffy. A tight board fence and a covered grandstand that could seat several thousand surrounded the baseball diamond. It was open to all baseball associations, the only rental being a percentage of gate and grandstand receipts. (Courtesy of David Barksdale.)

For years, Glenwood Park was the only real athletic field in the area, and it was always a busy place during the summer. In the fall, New Albany High School football games were played there until Buerk Field was established. (Courtesy of Stuart B. Wrege Indiana History Room.)

In June 1903, the newspapers carried stories of construction in Silver Creek Park. Stephen Day was given the contract for an open-air theater or pavilion. There would also be a covered dance floor. This postcard from 1908 shows the roller-skating rink at Glenwood Park. (Courtesy of David Barksdale.)

This carousel was one of the many attractions for children at Glenwood Park. In addition to the carousel, children could enjoy a Ferris wheel, a miniature train, and on special occasions, a circus. (Courtesy of Stuart B. Wrege Indiana History Room.)

In 1903, when Glenwood Park opened, Dr. John Baldwin of Jeffersonville envisioned it as an ideal location in which to introduce chautauqua to the surrounding area. He, with 10 other prominent men from New Albany and Jeffersonville, formed the Chautauqua Association. (Courtesy of Stuart B. Wrege Indiana History Room.)

Chautauqua was a traveling institution that was popular in the late 19th and early 20th centuries. It provided education, concerts, readings, dramatic performances, and even magicians. It was founded in Chautauqua, New York, and most often was presented outdoors or under a tent. (Courtesy of Stuart B. Wrege Indiana History Room.)

The first chautauqua debuted at Glenwood Park August 5–14, 1904, just one year after the park opened. This was considered the beginning of the golden age of culture. (Courtesy of Stuart B. Wrege Indiana History Room.)

William Jennings Bryan, whom many called the "silver-tongued orator," three times an unsuccessful candidate for president of the United States, opened the 10-day Chautauqua assembly. Also featured in that first series was May Wright Sewell. At various times in the 1890s, she had served as president of the National Council of Women and as chair of the executive committee of the Women's Suffrage Association. (Courtesy of Stuart B. Wrege Indiana History Room.)

An area was set aside in Glenwood Park for a "tent city." Families would rent tents and camp out for the duration of the Chautauqua. (Courtesy of Stuart B. Wrege Indiana History Room.)

ASSEMBLY TENT, CHAUTAUQUA, GLENWOOD PARK

A large tent, which seated 3,000 and was equipped with electric fans, was erected in the Glenwood Park Athletic Field beyond the baseball diamond, toward the creek. (Courtesy of Stuart B. Wrege Indiana History Room.)

Wood floors for tents could be built by the park carpenters, and stools and blankets could be rented. A list of boardinghouses and hotels was also available for those coming from the surrounding towns who did not wish to camp out. (Courtesy of Stuart B. Wrege Indiana History Room.)

Glenwood Park had all the comforts of home, including mail, which would be delivered daily if addressed in care of A. Heimburger, superintendent of the Chautauqua Association. There was also a safety patrol. These special police guarded the grounds day and night. Bells announced quiet time, which lasted until 6:00 a.m. The safety patrol would come around at 7:00 a.m. to check tickets. A season ticket cost $2.50. (Courtesy of Stuart B. Wrege Indiana History Room.)

During the season, Glenwood Park provided various refined attractions by well-known artists and famous bands. Public dances were held on certain days of the week, with other days reserved for private ones. (Courtesy of Stuart B. Wrege Indiana History Room.)

This 1915 photograph shows Dreyer's Concert Band, one of the most popular bands of the time. Professor Dreyer was a native of Indiana and played Glenwood Park many times throughout his career. He owned a music studio at Ninth and Main Streets in New Albany. (Courtesy of Stuart B. Wrege Indiana History Room.)

In 1909, Wilbery Embe played Nanki Poo in the summer Chautauqua Assembly opera production of *The Mikado*. (Courtesy of Stuart B. Wrege Indiana History Room.)

Opera companies and Shakespearean groups added a touch of high culture to the programs at the Chautauqua Assembly. This 1909 photograph shows a few cast members of *The Mikado* from the summer Chautauqua. (Courtesy of Stuart B. Wrege Indiana History Room.)

Glenwood Park offered many amusements intended for every walk of life. It was a place for recreation, which included baseball and dancing. Lovers of music could also find entertainment in listening to the bands of Sousa, Wagner, and Liberatti. For the more education-minded visitors, there was the Chautauqua event. (Courtesy of Stuart B. Wrege Indiana History Room.)

Chautauqua brought many nationally known speakers to Glenwood Park, including socialist Eugene Debs, evangelist Billy Sunday, and Thomas Marshall, a Democrat running for governor of Indiana. Some years later, Marshall spoke again at Glenwood Park when he was a candidate for vice president of the United States. (Courtesy of Stuart B. Wrege Indiana History Room.)

Glenwood Park consisted of two areas that made up the entire park. One was the athletic area with bleachers, a baseball diamond, and a football field. The other, the park proper, included the merry-go-round, Ferris wheel, bandstand, refreshment stand, fountain, pavilion, and miniature railroad traversing the park. (Courtesy of Stuart B. Wrege Indiana History Room.)

Glenwood Chautauqua 1914

Pictured here in 1913 is the Tri-Mu Club tent at the Chautauqua assembly in Glenwood Park. (Courtesy of Stuart B. Wrege Indiana History Room.)

Glenwood Park was a popular picnic area for schools, Sunday schools, graduations, clubs, and organizations hosting a summer gathering. The largest picnic—the Retail Grocers Picnic—was held annually in August and September. This event started in 1912 and was followed by another annual picnic, the Farmers and Merchants Jubilee, which started in 1917. (Courtesy of Stuart B. Wrege Indiana History Room.)

The Louisville & Southern Indiana Traction Company maintained the park from 1903 to 1921. By that time, the park had more than accomplished its goal of getting people to ride the interurban. This postcard shows people rowing in Silver Creek below the Louisville & Southern Indiana Traction Company bridge. (Courtesy of Stuart B. Wrege Indiana History Room.)

This photograph shows the miniature train ride at Glenwood Park. A train locomotive is hanging from a tree while track is being constructed. The miniature railroad had a track around the park, and would pass the pavilion, bowling alley, merry-go-round, Ferris wheel, and bandstand. (Courtesy of Stuart B. Wrege Indiana History Room.)

There was a sudden and severe thunderstorm in 1908, and the heavy winds caused the collapse of the tent. There were 2,000 people inside at the time, and although they were drenched and some sustained minor injuries, no one was killed. One of the leading performers at the Chautauqua event, Earl Hedden, was substituting for a no-show act at the time, and he later loved to tell of the time he "brought down the house." (Courtesy of Stuart B. Wrege Indiana History Room.)

This 1921 photograph shows the Retail Grocers Picnic. The grocers would display their specialties, raffle baskets of groceries, and give out free samples. These picnics lasted several days, and all the while, there were shows to be seen, bands to be heard, and dancing to be enjoyed. These extravaganzas brought out thousands of people and were held annually for many years. (Courtesy of Stuart B. Wrege Indiana History Room.)

Upon opening, Glenwood Park was a resort area, a place for recreation and entertainment. It soon became a source of culture and education when the Chautauqua was in session. This couple enjoys a stroll along the footbridge leading into the park. (Courtesy of Stuart B. Wrege Indiana History Room.)

Unfortunately, the flood of 1937 hit Glenwood Park as well as much of the Kentuckiana area hard. Note the water covering the streets and the rowboats sitting among the trees. (Courtesy of Stuart B. Wrege Indiana History Room.)

# *Four*

# WHITE CITY

White City was a common name for amusement parks across the United States, inspired by a nickname for the World's Columbian Exhibition of 1893. In 1901, Coney Island was the first to feature smaller parks—Luna Park, White City, and Electric Park—under its amusement park umbrella. A typical White City park featured a Shoot the Chutes and lagoon, a roller coaster, a midway, a Ferris wheel, games, and a pavilion. The White City in Kentuckiana only operated for five years. Following a massive fire in 1910 and subsequent rebuilding, White City, renamed Riverview Park, was unable to compete with the larger Fontaine Ferry and was forced to close after the 1912 season. The land was then sold for residential development a decade later. (Author's collection.)

For just 10¢, visitors could enter White City Amusement Park and spend the evening enjoying the sights, rides, and free band concerts that were offered. Featured here is the most iconic and

popular ride—Shoot the Chutes. (Courtesy of John Urbanavage.)

Live music at White City in 1907 included free band concerts every afternoon and evening. In addition to the live music, White City offered 30 special features for visitors to enjoy while at the park. (Courtesy of John Findling.)

This advertisement announced Cora Youngblood Corson and her band of world-famous all-girl instrumentalists from the West. The band played two concerts at White City on Saturday, June 8, 1907. (Courtesy of John Urbanavage.)

White City was located on Greenwood Avenue, south of Chickasaw Park, on the Ohio River and opened April 27, 1907. The park, known for its impressively ornate white buildings, was lit by 250,000 electric lights. (Courtesy of John Finding.)

Frederick Ingersoll, roller coaster designer and entrepreneur, provided many of the White City amusement parks with their roller coasters, which were either a figure eight or a scenic railway. (Courtesy of John Findling.)

White City was frequently billed as "the city of a million electric lights." A main feature of the park was a tall, brilliantly illuminated tower that could be seen for 15 miles. Unfortunately, because of these lights, many White City parks had fires, and during the summer season of 1910, the White City in Louisville caught fire. Unable to keep up with Fontaine Ferry just down the street, White City reopened in 1911 under the name Riverview Park but would not open again for the 1913 season. (Courtesy of John Urbanavage.)

White City took its name from the architectural style popularized by the 1893 World's Columbian Exposition. In this photograph, a Ferris wheel and a portion of the roller coaster can be seen behind the entrance, as well as a small portion of the lagoon and train track. (Courtesy of John Urbanavage.)

# *Five*

# Fontaine Ferry Park

The most iconic amusement park in Kentuckiana was Fontaine Ferry Park. Operating from 1905 to 1969, not only was it the longest-surviving amusement park in the area, it was considered the most popular and the largest of its kind. Fontaine Ferry Park was located on 64 acres in western Louisville along the Ohio River. The park offered over 50 rides and attractions as well as a swimming pool, skating rink, and theater. The most popular attraction was its wooden roller coaster, lovingly remembered by most visitors as "the Comet," even though three more coasters were built on the property over the years. The land that Fontaine Ferry sat on was originally part of Aaron Fontaine's estate and the ferry landing he had purchased in 1814. The property was sold in 1887 to Thomas Landenwich, who built a hotel and a few attractions. In May 1905, Park Circuit Realty Company, along with Landenwich, opened Fontaine Ferry Park. In 1917, Park Circuit Realty appointed Jefferson County judge Charles A. Wilson to manage the amusement park property. Benjamin G. Brinkman followed Judge Wilson, then John F. Singhiser, who created Fontaine Ferry Enterprises and was succeeded by son John "Jack" Singhiser as the last general manager. Visitors used steamboats to reach the park until the 1940s, after which trolleys and automobiles provided transportation from downtown Louisville. (Author's collection.)

Shawnee Park was a neighborhood in western Louisville that eventually became part of Fontaine Ferry. The broad meadow of Shawnee Park provided the ideal open site for recreation. Frederick Law Olmsted set out to design the park around the site's natural beauty. Trees were planted to frame the view of the Ohio River in addition to promenade beaches for swimming and a boat ramp for water access. These two women enjoy the beach on a sunny day at Shawnee Park. (Courtesy of Andy Albatys.)

Tony Landenwich purchased Fontaine's Ferry in 1887 and established the Fontaine Hotel and Restaurant. John Willard, the designer of Palisades Park in New York, conceived the idea of Fontaine Ferry Park. The owners, the Park Circuit Realty Company, began building the amusement park in 1903 and held its grand opening in May 1905. These two ladies stand in front of a billboard showing one of the many events hosted at Fontaine Ferry Park. (Courtesy of Andy Albatys.)

Fontaine Ferry Park opened in May 1905 and provided entertainment and excitement for children and adults. In addition to the usual rides and games, the park offered a 3,500-seat theater and a roller coaster called the Scenic Railway. There was also a bicycle track with a grandstand similar to Churchill Downs where major races were held. (Courtesy of Scott Allen.)

This card is from one of the early years at Fontaine Ferry Park. In an effort to promote the park in 1909, Fontaine Ferry planned to raffle off this goat and wagon. (Courtesy of Scott Allen.)

Visitors could sit in an automobile in front of a painted backdrop depicting a road to Louisville for a photo opportunity at Fontaine Ferry Park. (Author's collection.)

Fontaine Ferry Park was an instant success and became one of the nation's most famous parks. Many tried to open similar parks around the country. White City Amusement Park, just down the street, opened in 1907 but failed to compete with the larger park. This postcard shows the popularity of Fontaine Ferry Park as visitors stroll along the midway. (Author's collection.)

A World War I solider poses for a picture in his uniform while visiting Fontaine Ferry Park. (Author's collection.)

The *Idlewild*, a ferry excursion steamer, was launched on October 8, 1914, and for the first 10 years, operated primarily as a ferry between Memphis, Tennessee, and Arkansas. When the *Idlewild* was originally built, her hull was 157 feet long, 36 feet wide, and 5 feet deep. The maximum capacity was 1,600 passengers. (Courtesy of Barbara Montgomery.)

The *Idlewild* began making excursion tours carrying tourists in 1925. Having been originally chartered by the Rose Island Company in Charlestown, Indiana, the *Idlewild* arrived at Louisville in 1931. She ran trips from Fontaine Ferry in downtown Louisville upriver 14 miles to Rose Island. This picture shows the *Idlewild* at the Fontaine Ferry Landing, which predated the first Ohio River Bridge by 70 years. (Courtesy of Barbara Montgomery.)

This photograph was taken in January 1936 and shows the snow-covered automobile entrance to Fontaine Ferry Park. (Courtesy of Gary Matheis.)

The majority of visitors arrived to the park by steamboat, especially before automobile transportation was widely available. The steamboats would dock at a small Market Street beach along the Ohio River. With the city's first trolley car beginning operation in June 1889, plans were made to convert the mule-powered streetcar lines to electric. The switch produced a revolution in public transportation. Crowds increased at Fontaine Ferry Park once trolley lines were introduced; it was the turnaround point for the Market Street trolley line. (Courtesy of Gary Matheis.)

In the early days of Fontaine Ferry Park, visitors arrived by horse-drawn carriages and steamboats. Some made the trip on foot and later by streetcars and automobiles. The automobile age dawned in Louisville on October 4, 1898, when the first self-propelled, electrically powered vehicle arrived in the city. (Courtesy of Gary Matheis.)

John Miller, the architect of Palisades Park in New Jersey, was commissioned to design a grand-scale amusement park on the Shawnee Park property. The grand front entrance originally featured twin towers and was nearly five stories tall. This view of the Louisville landmark shows the towers removed and admission booth enlarged. (Courtesy of Gary Matheis.)

Many rides came and went over the years. Famous rides included the Tilt-A-Whirl, Lindy Planes, Rocket, Ferris wheel, Loop-the-Loop, Whip, Caterpillar, Loop-O-Planes, Paratrooper, Bubble Bounce, Turnpike, and Skooters. Featured in this photograph is the Lindy Plane. (Courtesy of Gary Matheis.)

A World War II solider enjoys a ride on the Lindy Planes, named after Charles Lindbergh. The Lindy Planes were removed in 1946 to make way for the Rocket. (Courtesy of Gary Matheis.)

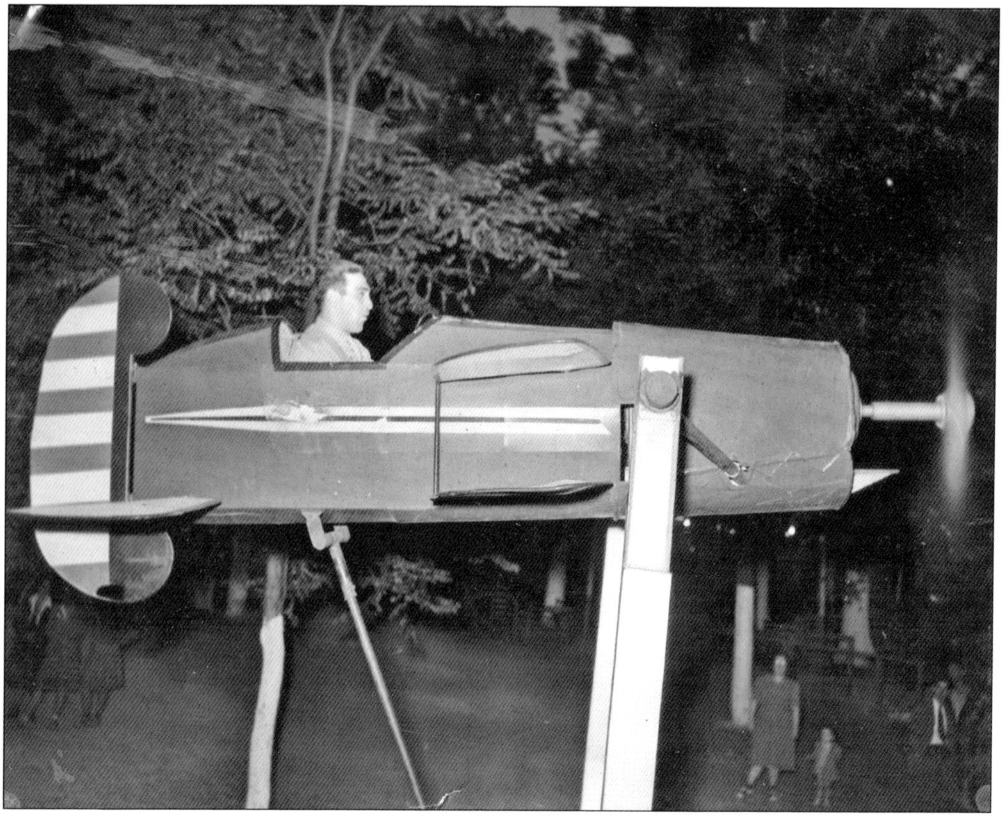

Many adults had just as much fun at Fontaine Ferry Park as the children. This photograph shows a man riding a Lindy Plane. (Courtesy of Gary Matheis.)

Two park employees stand next to the Loop-O-Planes ride. The small car was shaped like a plane and attached to a tall pole. (Courtesy of Gary Matheis.)

A somewhat uninterested employee keeps watch over the Loop-O-Planes ride as it loops around. (Courtesy of Gary Matheis.)

In addition to the thrilling rides, there were areas in the park that entertained visitors, including Puzzle Town, Mystery Town, Mirror Maze, and Kiddieland. (Courtesy of Gary Matheis.)

These four girls are having the time of their lives spinning around on the Tilt-a-Whirl ride at Fontaine Ferry Park. (Courtesy of Gary Matheis.)

This young lady, Nora, worked at Skooters, a bumper car game originally called Dodge 'em Cars. (Courtesy of Gary Matheis.)

The Turnpike was a very popular attraction at Fontaine Ferry Park. With no real track, one could steer the car within the lane, although drivers were encouraged not to bump into others. Prior to the Turnpike, the Olde Mill, later the Tunnel of Love, sat near the entrance of the park. Youngsters trailed their hands in the water, while the older "youngsters" took their best boys or girls for a ride. There were many stories that claimed the waters were snake infested. (Courtesy of Scott Allen.)

A fond memory of many children after riding one of the roller coasters at the park was when the roller coaster operator would announce the re-ride option at the end for 10¢. Many recall his loud, drawling voice. (Courtesy of Gary Matheis.)

The Paratrooper ride was one of the popular attractions at Fontaine Ferry Park. It was a revolving swing-seat ride and is still operating at Knoebel's Amusement Park in Pennsylvania. (Courtesy of Gary Matheis.)

Fontaine Ferry Park had 50 rides, so there was something for everyone—fast roller coasters and the Paratrooper for thrill seekers or slower-paced attractions like one of the fun houses. Many fondly remember the summers they spent at the park with their friends. (Courtesy of Gary Matheis.)

Fontaine Ferry proudly sported four roller coasters through the years. The Comet was the last of the great coasters, built in 1951, and was the fastest in its day. This photograph shows the owners and employees on the Comet's first run. The coaster became stuck on the track that day, and this group had to abandon the cars and walk back along the tracks. (Courtesy of Gary Matheis.)

To some, the Comet roller coaster, with no real restraints, was deemed too terrifying to ride. Many people rode the coasters standing up, and a few took an unexpected flight. The concrete footings that once supported the coaster can still be seen on the property today. (Courtesy of Scott Allen.)

There were four wooden roller coasters in the park's history. The original Scenic Railway (1905–1910), the Racing Derby (1910–1936), the Velvet Racer (1936–1945), and the breathtaking Comet (1951–1968). The Comet featured a 90-foot drop and 3,800 feet of track. (Courtesy of Gary Matheis.)

Loop-the-Loop was the first wooden roller coaster, but it was destined to have a short lifetime due to its poor design and capacity issues. The Loop-the-Loop coexisted with the Scenic Railway, a John Miller design built by Fred Ingersoll that closed in 1910. The Scenic Railway was replaced by the Racing Derby, which thrilled riders for 26 years. When it came time to replace the Racing Derby, Miller had his own company and supplied the Velvet Racer. (Courtesy of Gary Matheis.)

The Velvet Racer suffered through two of the worst floods in Louisville history, including the 1937 flood. Luckily, the rest of Fontaine Ferry was unaffected by the 1937 flood. The skating rink was actually used by the Red Cross during the flood. (Courtesy of Gary Matheis.)

Being so near the Ohio River, this roller coaster was flooded by the water. The Velvet Racer was replaced and became the Comet, a fan favorite. (Courtesy of Gary Matheis.)

Hilarity Hall, a fun house at Fontaine Ferry Park, was home to either fond memories or nightmares for visitors greeted by the animated laughing Sam and Sal. Sam and Sal remained at Fontaine Ferry Park until it closed in 1969. They were then sold in an auction to an Oklahoma amusement park. Unfortunately, the two caught fire before the park could put them on display. (Courtesy of Gary Matheis.)

Two girls enjoy ice cream while playing in Hilarity Hall. Also included in Hilarity Hall were the ever-rolling barrel, the sugar bowl, and the double slides. (Courtesy of Gary Matheis.)

The double slides were also known as the devil and angel slides. The angel slide was longer and not quite as dangerous or scary as the devil slide. (Courtesy of Scott Allen.)

Hilarity Hall had something for everyone. There were sliding floors, one side to side and another forward and backward. There was an air hole in the floor, which would blow an unsuspecting girl's dress up as she crossed over it. The silly mirrors made visitors appear large, skinny, short, and otherwise goofy. There was an ever-rolling barrel, where many would fall while trying to walk through. Other visitors would spread their hands and feet apart and would turn over and over inside. (Courtesy of Scott Allen.)

Most families in the neighborhood received a pass to get in the gates of Fontaine Ferry, and visitors only paid for the rides they rode. On Wednesdays, the price of some of the rides dropped to a nickel, and on Pepsi Day, the liner from a Pepsi-Cola bottle cap was good for a discount on many of the attractions. (Courtesy of Gary Matheis.)

Another popular activity was the Rockin' Horses, a carousel-type horse ride that moved forward and back. (Courtesy of Gary Matheis.)

County days were popular events at the park. Certain days of the week would be set aside for a particular county. There was also Pepsi Day. There was always plenty of popcorn and cotton candy to go around. (Courtesy of Gary Matheis.)

Many neighborhood kids were employed at Fontaine Ferry Park. This image shows, from left to right, Florene Murphy, John Sampel, and Hubert Rogens posing during a break. At one point, Fontaine Ferry had 250 summer employees, with an extra 75 on the weekends. (Courtesy of Gary Matheis.)

A favorite of many children was the penny arcade. This area had games of chance, a shooting gallery, a fishpond, and more. Favorite penny arcade games included an electric cowboy quick-draw machine and a machine with a crank and handle to flip pages of an illustration to simulate a moving picture. Many events were also held inside the penny arcade, such as this display of soap box derby cars. (Courtesy of Gary Matheis.)

This 1930s photograph shows a group of onlookers excited to see the debut of a new automobile. The Louisville Automobile Club showed cars at Fontaine Ferry Park during its midsummer show. (Courtesy of Gary Matheis.)

This photograph shows a 1933 bathing beauty contest held at Fontaine Ferry Park. Company names can be seen on some of the girl's sashes. (Courtesy of Gary Matheis.)

Thousands of visitors crowded the park grounds on summer weekends, with attendance significantly increasing during special annual promotions such as county days, nickel days, and well-attended company picnics. (Courtesy of Gary Matheis.)

In 1947, last owner Jack Singhiser formed Fontaine Ferry Enterprises. Here, Singhiser holds court with a group of people near the old grape arbor at round tables and chairs in the shade of the huge trees. Many families visiting the park would sit and eat and drink together at these tables. There was beer for the men, coffee for the ladies, and milk or soda pop for the children. (Courtesy of Gary Matheis.)

Pappy Aubrey operated a roller coaster at Fontaine Ferry Park before it became River Glen Park. Aubrey began work at the park when he was about 13, raking leaves. The park installed a Racing Derby ride in 1910, and Aubrey was asked to operate it. He helped operate all the roller coasters and almost every morning took a spin on them "just to see if they were working right." (Courtesy of Gary Matheis.)

There were skating clubs that would use the Fontaine Ferry Park skating rink for organized programs and competitions. There were also benefit shows at the skating rink with sometimes as many as 65 skaters in one program. (Courtesy of Gary Matheis.)

The skating rink was very popular during the Great Depression, when walk-a-thons were hosted there. The grand prize winner could walk away with a $75 bedroom set, with secondary prizes of $25. This couple received a skating competition trophy. (Courtesy of Gary Matheis.)

One of the most popular attractions at Fontaine Ferry was the magical and majestic carousel. It was built by one of the country's foremost carousel builders, the Dentzel Carousel Company, in the late 1880s. Dentzel carousels were known for their realistic and graceful animals with elaborate carvings. The carousel at Fontaine Ferry featured several different kinds of animals, jesters, cupids, and decorative scenes. (Courtesy of Scott Allen.)

Free band concerts were performed at Fontaine Ferry Park every afternoon and evening. The Cook Military Band performed on August 4, 1906, while visiting the summer theater in the park. (Author's collection.)

When the Fontaine Ferry Park Theatre opened with its 3,500 seats, it was a multi-purpose building that sometimes featured professional basketball games and prize fights. Three times a day, a national or local act of magicians, performing dogs, or musicians would perform a variety show from the stage. (Courtesy of Gary Matheis.)

The outdoor stage had row after row of green park benches. Visitors had to get to the shows early for a choice seat. (Courtesy of Gary Matheis.)

The Ferris wheel was reportedly moved to Bell's Amusement Park in Tulsa, Oklahoma, after Fontaine Ferry Park closed. In recent years, it was reported the Ferris wheel was destroyed by a tornado. (Courtesy of Gary Matheis.)

Jack Singhiser kept a photo album of employees and friends from the park. A Ferris wheel operator is featured in this picture. (Courtesy of Gary Matheis.)

There are few winter photographs of Fontaine Ferry Park. This image of Gypsy Village was taken in January while the park was closed. Constructed in 1936, Gypsy Village was an outdoor dance garden with an indoor theater. In later years, the theater was converted into the indoor dance garden seen here. (Courtesy of Gary Matheis.)

The German-style beer garden was another popular attraction for older visitors. Many recall the white tables under the shade of the white-washed trees in the middle of a dozen major thrill rides. (Courtesy of Gary Matheis.)

Starting as a dance garden with an indoor theater, Gypsy Village housed all kinds of music. Guests could even hear opera in Gypsy Village. Eventually, the theater became a dance hall with performers like Perry Como, the Tommy Dorsey Band, John Philip Sousa's band, the Dunbar Light Opera Company, Mary Pickford, Will Rogers, Fred Astaire, and Louis Armstrong making appearances. (Courtesy of Gary Matheis.)

Gypsy Village featured many local and national bands. Famous acts like the Sultans, Jackie Wilson, Chet Cline, Randy Atcher and Cactus, Ginger Calahan, Johnny Burkarth and his orchestra, and even a young Frank Sinatra took the stage at Gypsy Village. (Courtesy of Gary Matheis.)

Gypsy Village was a nightclub primarily for adults, a place to enjoy beer and live music and dancing. Many national acts toured Gypsy Village for the dances on Saturday and Sunday nights. Gypsy Village was open to teens once a week. (Courtesy of Gary Matheis.)

In the days of the big bands, Stan Kenton attracted 2,600 people in one night—a record that still stands. These folks are enjoying beer and live music in Gypsy Village. (Courtesy of Gary Matheis.)

Adults who visited Fontaine Ferry often remember hanging out at Gypsy Village enjoying beers with friends. On occasion, teenagers were able to sneak in. Many teenage boys could get in if they could dance well. These employees enjoy a drink at the end of a workday—after hours, of course. (Courtesy of Gary Matheis.)

Throughout Fontaine Ferry Park, there was pea gravel on the ground and the trunks of the trees were painted white. Most of the outdoor furniture, structures, and a few rides were made of wood. The outdoor pavilion of Gypsy Village was a very romantic spot for couples to go and listen to music and dance together. (Courtesy of Scott Allen.)

The neighboring Aubrey Dude Ranch operated a pony ride for young children wanting to be cowboys and cowgirls. There was even a "Rawhide" western character who would lead the ponies around the track. There was also a Riding Academy for the more experienced cowboys and cowgirls. (Courtesy of Gary Matheis.)

Aubrey Dude Ranch was near Fontaine Ferry Park, with stables close to Shawnee Park. The track and trails were on Fontaine Ferry property and ran from Market Street to the south of Shawnee Park. The ranch remained in operation until it was sold in 1983. (Courtesy of Gary Matheis.)

The swimming pool, complete with a cascading waterfall, was second in size only to Louisville's Crescent Hill pool, even though Fontaine Ferry Park advertised it as the largest. (Courtesy of Gary Matheis.)

The pool was the place to be on hot summer days. This group of friends takes a moment to pose poolside. The Olympic-sized swimming pool featured a slide, high dive, waterfall, overhead walkway to observe swimmers, and a wooden wheel ride. (Courtesy of Gary Matheis.)

The swimming pool was constructed on the site of the former Scenic Railway in 1915, 10 years after the park opened. This waterslide was later added to the swimming pool, and throngs of people enjoyed it. (Courtesy of Gary Matheis.)

At times, a rope divided the pool at the four-foot mark. Visitors had to prove to the lifeguards they could swim by going across and back before being allowed in the deep end with the high dive and slide. (Courtesy of Gary Matheis.)

The swimming pool was constructed on the site of the former Scenic Railway in 1915, ten years after the park was opened. Painted on the western wall of the pool area was a sign that read, "Gentlemen will. Others must behave." (Courtesy of Gary Matheis.)

The wooden wheel ride that was later a feature of the Fontaine Ferry Park pool can be seen in this photograph of the Ohio River. The main swimming area prior to the opening of the pool was the Shawnee Bathing Beach. The building at the top of the beach used as a bathing house was moved farther onto the property in 1936 and converted into Gypsy Village. Had the building not been moved in 1936, it would have likely been swept away by the flood of 1937. (Courtesy of Gary Matheis.)

The pool house has been linked to launching the career of the late Tim Krekel, a Louisville musician who reportedly played on the pool house roof for 35¢. (Courtesy of Gary Matheis.)

This rare photograph of the high dive at the swimming pool shows an employee siting on the edge of the diving board during the off-season. (Courtesy of Gary Matheis.)

A park nurse, here referred to as "Mac," was on duty at Fontaine Ferry Park. (Courtesy of Gary Matheis.)

Also on staff at Fontaine Ferry were several guards and patrol officers. (Courtesy of Gary Matheis.)

The Marvelous Mystery House is seen here during a rare break from the crowds. Guests could tour it for just 12¢. (Courtesy of Gary Matheis.)

Attendance soared sky-high on discount days. The park frequently hosted county days, nickel days, and Pepsi Day, and always had free parking. Coupons were frequently printed in the *Louisville Times*. (Courtesy of Gary Matheis.)

The park was never at a loss for action. This opening season advertisement for Fontaine Ferry Park in 1969 referred to it as Louisville's million-dollar playland with free stage shows, a swimming pool, 51 big rides and attractions, and plenty of picnic tables to enjoy snacks and beverages. (Courtesy of Gary Matheis.)

Unfortunately, Fontaine Ferry Park was not fun for everyone. While many have pleasant memories of the park, there are just as many who do not remember it so fondly. It is truly unfortunate that the park was not open to everyone, since it was segregated until 1963. Some visitors remember a line extending from the fence across the entranceway marking the private property of the park, and those who were not welcome who crossed the line were arrested for trespassing. (Author's collection.)

According to a 1961 article in the *Louisville Times*, protesters began to gather in front of the huge gates, demanding to share in the fun inside. On several nights, there were mass demonstrations outside the main entrance, and there were numerous arrests. (Courtesy of Scott Allen.)

Fontaine Ferry Park remained segregated until May 5, 1964. Even then, however, the pool was still segregated. A case was brought to court to enforce the city's public accommodation law, and segregation at the pool ended in 1965. (Courtesy of Scott Allen.)

After segregation ended, the park operated without any major issues until the opening day of May 4, 1969, when a fight turned into a near riot, and the owners decided they could not operate the park safely. (Courtesy of Scott Allen.)

The *Louisville Times* ran an article the day after the riot on May 5, 1969, about the fate of Fontaine Ferry Park. Jack Singhiser, the park's president, said that "the definite possibility of a reoccurrence" of the previous night's riot led to the decision to close the park. (Courtesy of Scott Allen.)

The opening day at Fontaine Ferry Park in 1969 was also the final closing day. The riot that day caused a lot of destruction and raised issues with security. On the following day, Jack Singhiser announced that Fontaine Ferry Park would close for good. (Courtesy of Gary Matheis.)

With over $18,000 in damages, workers injured, and money stolen during the riot, Jack Singhiser decided to close Fontaine Ferry Park. Nephew Jim Singhiser recalls his uncle was devastated. Rides and machines from the penny arcade were sold. Jack Singhiser even took the wiring out of the ground to sell the copper. This photograph features, from left to right, John Singhiser, son Jack Singhiser, and assistant manager Bill Matheis. (Courtesy of Gary Matheis.)

Two days after the park closed on May 6, 1969, the park directors met and decided they could no longer operate the park successfully. An estimated 2,000 people were in the park when the trouble reached its peak at about 8:00 p.m. About 55 policemen were summoned. (Courtesy of Gary Matheis.)

In an article from the *Louisville Times*, Metropolitan Parks director Charlie Vettiner said he was interested in the possibility of incorporating Fontaine Ferry into the city-county park system. Vettiner planned to bring the Fontaine Ferry Park closing before the Metropolitan Park Board at its next meeting on May 22 to propose leasing for the pool for the summer. (Courtesy of Gary Matheis.)

The pool was drained and left in limbo, and Fontaine Ferry Park sat as a ghost town during what should have been the 1969 summer season. (Courtesy of Gary Matheis.)

The roller-skating rink, Gypsy Village dance garden, and swimming pool were also closed. Singhiser said the park and its equipment were worth about $1.5 million and would be sold. (Courtesy of Gary Matheis.)

Metropolitan Parks director Charlie Vettiner reported he was not interested in the roller coaster and other rides at the park, but felt that the picnic facilities gave Fontaine Ferry plenty of possibilities as a public park. (Courtesy of Gary Matheis.)

Fontaine Ferry Park, seemingly frozen in time, was left empty at the would-be start of a bustling summer season. The *Star West Louisville* newspaper noted that the Hot Dog on a Stick played second fiddle to a cash register as looters ripped the register apart and placed the drawer on the counter. (Courtesy of Gary Matheis.)

After the closing of Fontaine Ferry in 1969, the park was purchased by National Services Industries of Atlanta. The park reopened as Ghost Town on the River in 1972. (Courtesy of Gary Matheis.)

In an article from the *Louisville Times*, new manager Daniel M. Brown is quoted as saying, "We've got to let Louisville know we're back. The name Ghost Town doesn't mean anything to anyone. People don't realize it's old Fontaine Ferry Park." (Courtesy of Scott Allen.)

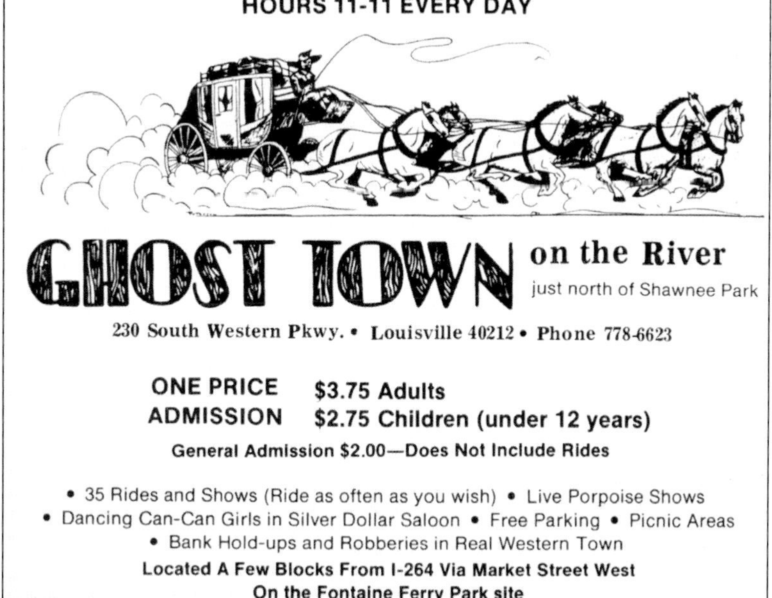

The National Recreation Service, a brand of National Services Industries, purchased Fontaine Ferry Park. The reported purchase price for the park was $299,000, but the National Services Industries spokesperson said that was not the entire cost and did not give the full amount. Pictured is the famous Fontaine Ferry Park entryway as it stood in 1976. (Courtesy of Jason Rayburn.)

Ghost Town on the River was managed by Daniel M. Brown. The transition from Fontaine Ferry Park was not as smooth as hoped. The company reportedly lost $450,00 just on operations. It spent $2 million on renovations and equipment in addition to another $1 million for new paint, flowers, and restored fountains. The new owners also updated the food stands and added restrooms. (Courtesy of Johnny Urbanavage.)

On May 25, 1976, the main gates and the penny arcade caught fire from a spark and burned down. After the fire, many of the remaining rides were sold to various locations around the country. The beloved carousel is still intact and presently located at Six Flags Great America near Chicago. (Courtesy of Gary Matheis.)

River Glen Park was put on the auction block in 1975. The auction sold such items as 1,100 feet of split rail fence, wooden horses from the merry-go-round, garden hose, and wheelbarrows. There were also 25 buildings on the property that were to be removed. (Courtesy of Johnny Urbanavage.)

The firm auctioning the property had been trying to get $650,000 for land that was called a "million-dollar piece of property." However, the auctioneer took the land off the market when the highest bid came to only $130,000 for the 62 acres. The Comet was eventually torn down. This is one of the last photographs of the roller coaster. (Courtesy of Johnny Urbanavage.)

# *Six*

# Kiddieland

In a WLKY commercial, Kiddieland advertised "All the world's a stage, and all the men and women may be players but for the small fry, a pretty afternoon and an amusement park primarily designed for children are what makes the stage for little actors and actresses." Kiddieland Amusement Park was one of the two major amusement parks in the Louisville area, but it was the only one that catered to children. It was located near the corner of Berry Boulevard at 3525 South Seventh Street. Memorable rides included a fire truck ride, a Ferris wheel, a junior-sized roller coaster called the Little Dipper, a merry-go-round, a miniature train ride, a boat ride, and a pony track. Kiddieland opened in the early 1960s and was renamed Funland Park in 1965. It enticed visitors with reduced rates for groups and plenty of free parking. Unfortunately, very few quality photographs of Kiddieland remain. Commercial ads offer the best remaining views of the park. (Author's collection.)

Specializing in rides and amusements for young children, Kiddieland sent letters to schools with end-of-the-year offers. It advertised as a place to hold class outings, with free parking, free admission, discount rates on all ride tickets to school groups, free picnic tables and shelter in case of rain, 12 exciting rides plus live ponies, refreshment stands and souvenir novelties, areas enclosed for the protection of small children, and no rental charges. This is a hand-drawn illustration of a coupon for the newspaper offering a discount to visitors to Kiddieland. (Courtesy of Gary Matheis.)

A Kiddieland newspaper promotion advertised that the whole family could have fun at the park: "Bring the children to the happiest land of all, Kiddieland Amusement Park. This is Louisville's most popular play land for the Small Fry. Parents are welcome too; in fact you are in for a lot of fun just watching the children enjoy themselves in the fresh air and sunshine. Come one, come all and enjoy the fun." (Author's collection.)

Mrs. Snellex, a teacher at Parkland Elementary School, took some time to send this personal note of thanks to owner Bill Matheis for his kindness and for the fun time that the children had at Kiddieland. While the park was not as elaborate as Fontaine Ferry, many have fond memories of the times they spent at the park enjoying rides built especially for them. (Both, courtesy of Gary Matheis.)

Dear Mr. Matheis,

We want to thank-you for all the kindness you showed us while we were at Funland Park yesterday. Being five-year olds, we sometimes are a little rough, However, the experiences we received and the fun we had will surely make us more grown-up. We had a wonderful time and we hope we can come back someday again. Thank-you for letting us have so much fun.

Mrs. Snellex's headstart classes at Parkland Elem. School

COMMUNITY 5c DAY

KIDDIELAND AMUSEMENT PARK
7th St. ROAD NEAR BERRY

Sponsored By

BURGER CHEF SHIVELY NEWSWEEK

SATURDAY, AUG. 8th, NOON 'TIL ?

This Ticket and 5c good on any one of following rides

MERRY-GO-ROUND
FIRE TRUCK
MINIATURE TRAIN
LITTLE DIPPER

4

HAND CARS
BOATS
FERRIS WHEEL
SKY FIGHTER

Free Admission • Free Parking

Community 5¢ days were always very popular at Kiddieland. This coupon, sponsored by Burger Chef and the *Shively Newsweek*, enticed visitors to ride the merry-go-round, the fire truck ride, the miniature train, the Little Dipper, the hand cars, the boats, the Ferris wheel, and the Sky Fighter for 5¢ each. (Courtesy of Gary Matheis.)

REPUBLICAN 5c DAY

KIDDIELAND AMUSEMENT PARK
7th ST. ROAD NEAR BERRY

Sponsored By

SHIVELY REPUBLICAN ORGANIZATION

Saturday, Aug. 24, 1963, noon 'til ?

This Ticket and 5c good on any one of following rides:

MERRY-GO-ROUND
FIRE TRUCK
MINIATURE TRAIN
LITTLE DIPPER

HAND CARS
BOATS
FERRIS WHEEL
SKY FIGHTER

Free Admission • Free Parking

Kiddieland could also be rented for school trips, church picnics, or club meetings. Pictured here is a 5¢ coupon for the Shively Republican Organization. (Courtesy of Gary Matheis.)

Ask anyone who remembers Kiddieland and chances are they will talk about bottle cap day. Visitors were encouraged to save their bottle caps from Pepsi-Cola, Teem, and Patio Diet Cola in exchange for rides on Wednesdays at Kiddieland. Similar promotions were also held with the Canada Dry Bottling Company in Louisville. Visitors could enjoy free rides at Kiddieland when presenting a Tab bottle cap. (Courtesy of Gary Matheis.)

**SAVE**

**THESE BOTTLE CAPS**

**and**

**PATIO DIET COLA**

**...they're valuable for Kiddieland Rides!**

**GOOD EVERY WEDNESDAY**
**July 10th through August 28th**

**PEPSI'S NICKEL (5c) DAY**
**At**
**Kiddieland Amusement Park**
**7th Street Road at Berry Blvd.**

**Save your PEPSI-COLA, TEEM and PATIO DIET COLA caps because a cap and 5c will entitle you to enjoy these rides every Wednesday.**

Miniature Train
Merry-Go-Round
Boats
Ferris Wheel
Sky Fighter
Hand Cars
Little Dipper Roller Coaster
Fire Truck

No limit to number of caps redeemed.

*Now... it's Pepsi!*

**FREE**

**RIDES AT**

**KIDDIELAND**

**3525 7th ST. ROAD**

**WITH 1 STAR CARTON TAB**

ON THE

MERRY-GO-ROUND
FERRIS WHEEL
HAND CARS
FIRE TRUCK

**CANADA DRY BOTTLING CO.**

LOUISVILLE, KENTUCKY

Kiddieland offered a value pack for 50¢, which included one ride on the merry-go-round, Ferris wheel, fire truck, and boat rides. (Courtesy of Gary Matheis.)

KIDDIE RIDES
REFRESHMENTS

SPECIAL RATES FOR GROUPS
BIRTHDAYS CHURCHES

**APRIL 18 thru LABOR DAY 1964**

**KIDDIE LAND, INC.**
3525 7th St. Blvd.
Near Berry Blvd.
**For Further Information**
**Call 366-7748**

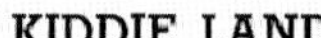

**KIDDIE LAND**

**The Whole Family Can Have Fun**

Bring the children to the happiest land of all . . . Kiddie Land Amusement Park. This is Louisville's most popular play land for the Small Fry. Parents are welcome too, in fact you are in for a lot of fun just watching the children enjoy themselves in the fresh air and sunshine.
Come One, Come All and enjoy the fun.

**VALUE 50c**

**KIDDIE RIDES**

"Be Our Guest" Passes Below Good Any Day April 18 Thru Labor Day, 1964, Except Special Party Days.
**KIDDIE LAND AMUSEMENT PARK**
**3525 7th St. Road Near Berry Blvd.**
Must Be Detached By Attendant

| Good For One Ride On Kiddie Merry-Go Round | Good For One Ride On Kiddie Ferris Wheel | Good For One Ride On Kiddie Fire Truck | Good For One Ride On Kiddie Boat Ride |
|---|---|---|---|

Kiddieland was renamed Funland Park in April 1965, and was advertised as "A Paradise for Fun." This flyer was sent to all kinds of groups encouraging them to have their annual picnics, employee picnics, or special outings at Funland Park. (Courtesy of Gary Matheis.)

PICNIC DETAILS

No Rental Charge for Picnics — Free Parking — Free Admission

| | |
|---|---|
| Operating Hours | — Weekdays — 2 p.m. till 10 p.m.<br>Saturday, Sundays & Holidays — 12 noon till 10 p.m.<br>(Different hours can be arranged for picnics) |
| Insurance | — Park Fully Covered by Liability Insurance<br>(Copy can be furnished any group desiring same) |
| Seating | — Picnic Tables and Benches located all over Park<br>(Refreshment building may be used in case of rain) |
| Food | — Picnic Groups may bring Food, with the exception of Soft Drinks & Beer |

FOOD AVAILABLE REFRESHMENT STAND:

| | | | |
|---|---|---|---|
| Beer | 25c | Hot Dogs | 25c |
| Pepsi | | Foot Long Hot Dogs | 35c |
| Root Beer | | Potato Chips | 10c |
| Orange & Grape | 10c - 20c | Snacks | 10c |
| Cotton Candy | 20c - 25c | Ice Cream | 10c |
| Popcorn | 15c - 25c | (Sandwiches & Sticks) | |
| Snow Balls | 15c | | |

SKILLED ATTENDANTS ON EACH RIDE

| | | | |
|---|---|---|---|
| TRAIN (Adults & Children) | 20c | SKY FIGHTER (Children Only) | 20c |
| LITTLE DIPPER COASTER (Adults & Children) | 20c | FIRE TRUCK (Adults & Children) | 15c |
| BIG FERRIS WHEEL (Adults & Children) | 25c | KIDDIE MERRY GO ROUND (Small Children) | 15c |
| TILT-A-WHIRL (Adults & Children) | 25c | BOATS (Children Only) | 20c |
| CAROUSEL (Adults & Children) | 20c | KIDDIE FERRIS WHEEL (Children Only) | 15c |
| HAND CARS (Children Only) | 15c | LIVE PONIES (Children Only) | 15c |

Special Prices on Rides to Picnic Groups, etc.
Tickets are Sold in 5c Denomination — 50c on a Strip

PRICES FOR PICNIC GROUPS:
Up To First $500.00 — $1.50 Worth of Tickets for $1.00
$500.00 Or More — $2.00 Worth of Ride Tickets for $1.00

PICNICS ARE BOOKED ON ANY DAY OF WEEK ON FIRST COME FIRST SERVED BASIS

GAMES MAY BE PLAYED IF DESIRED
(Such as Horseshoe Pitching, Three Legged Races, Fly Casting, Etc.)

ORGANIZATIONS MAY SET UP WHEELS IF DESIRED (Ham - Cake - Toys - Bacon, Etc.)

NO GAMBLING

All money taken in on wheels retained by organization — No accounting to Funland necessary.

Organizations may set up as many booths as desired, but a list must be submitted to Funland in advance.

Most rides at Funland Park ranged from 15¢ to 25¢ and included a train, Little Dipper coaster, regular-sized Ferris wheel and kiddie Ferris wheel, Tilt-a-Whirl, carousel, hand cars, Sky Fighter, fire truck, merry-go-round, boat rides, and live ponies. (Courtesy of Gary Matheis.)

Kiddieland frequently held community days and 5¢ days with various sponsors such as the Ranch House, Arlan's Department Store, Burger Chef, and the *Shively Newsweek*. During these discount days, rides cost only 5¢, except the pony ride and Turnpike. (Courtesy of Gary Mathies.)

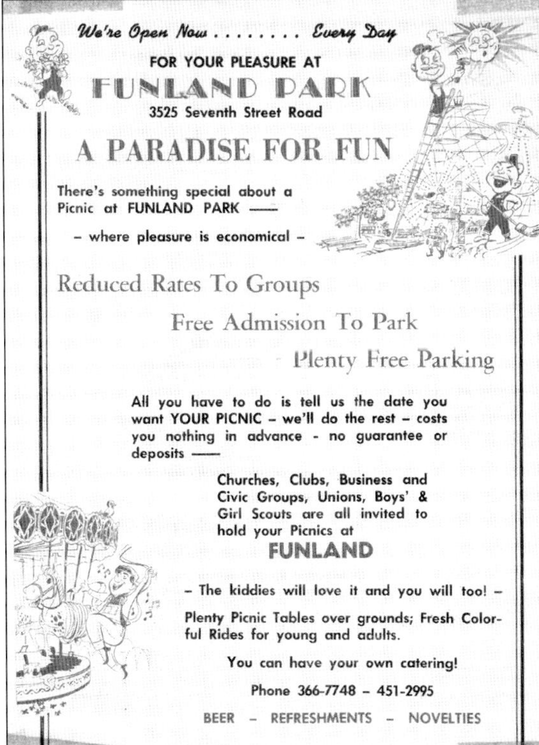


This full-page flyer advertises all the fun one could have seven days a week at 3525 Seventh Street Road. Kiddieland hosted clubs, picnics, churches, and other community organizations. Food, soft drinks, and beer were available at a refreshment stand, and picnic groups were encouraged to bring their own food, with the exception of soft drinks and beer. (Courtesy of Gary Matheis.)

ARLAN'S DEPARTMENT STORE

COURTESY COUPON FOR

1/2 PRICE ON RIDE TICKETS

AT

FUNLAND PARK

"Across The Street"

Take This Coupon To Funland Park

$2.00 WORTH OF RIDE TICKETS FOR $1.00

FREE ADMISSION GOOD SEASON 1967 FREE PARKING

Most visitors will also remember the popular Arlan's Department Store, located across the street from Kiddieland. Arlan's offered this discount coupon for half price on ride tickets. (Courtesy of Gary Matheis.)

"The Children's Own Land of Play"

OPEN EVERY DAY

Opening Times

SATURDAYS 12:00 (Noon)

SUNDAYS 10:00 a.m.

WEEKDAYS 5:00 p.m.

FUN!
EXCITEMENT!
REFRESHMENTS!
LAUGHS!

★ RIDE THE KIDDIE MERRY-GO-ROUND

★ LIVE PONY RIDE ★ KIDDIE FERRIS WHEEL

★ KIDDIE SKY FIGHTER ★ KIDDIE BOATS IN REAL WATER

★ MINIATURE STREAMLINED L. & N. TRAIN "THE LITTLE HUMMINGBIRD"

NO ADMISSION CHARGE TO PARK

LOCATED ON 7TH NEAR BERRY BOULEVARD
ENTRANCES ON BOTH—MAIN ENTRANCE ON 7TH

Kiddieland was open seven days a week, starting at 5:00 p.m. on weekdays. (Courtesy of Gary Matheis.)

# *Seven*

# What Remains Today

While these lost amusement parks are no longer operating, they are certainly not entirely forgotten. To this day, many people fondly remember the times they spent roaming the parks along both sides of the Ohio River. Most of the former park lands have been developed for residential properties or public parks. There are still a few small traces of these long-lost amusement parks. The most significant attempt to mark their history is at Rose Island in Charlestown State Park. Rose Island has undergone a recent resurgence thanks to the state park and the addition of a new walking bridge. When the grounds of Rose Island became the property of the Indiana Army Ammunitions Plant in the 1940s, it was completely closed off. Charlestown State Park was created in 1996 as part of the Federal Lands to Parks Program, and the state was given approximately 1,000 acres of the old ammunition plant, which included the Rose Island site. There was no direct access to Rose Island once the plant took over. Luckily, the state found some grants for the preservation of historic bridges and funded a project to move a historic bridge from Indiana to the site. (Author's collection.)

Visitors who take a walk from Trails 3 and 4 in Charlestown State Park across the new Portersville Bridge will arrive in Rose Island. The Vincennes Bridge Company of Vincennes, Indiana, built the bridge in 1911. Its construction is fairly uncommon; it is made of iron, which was used for less than 20 years and soon replaced by steel. The bridge was picked up from its original site and rebuilt at its current location at Rose Island. (Courtesy of Jeff Ketterman.)

A reproduction of the original sign, although much smaller, stands at the entrance to Rose Island with timeline panels and images of the old park. The original sign survived the 1937 flood and remained until the late 1970s, although no one knows what happened to it. Park rangers did find evidence that the poles were cut down and the sign taken. The park hopes that one day the sign will be returned to its original place at the entrance to the park. (Courtesy of Jeff Ketterman.)

The Walkway of Roses was restored with new columns and iron arches to show what it looked like when Rose Island was in its prime. Electric lights hung along the walkway in the 1920s. Today, the stones along the path have been restored to their original location, and the recreated columns give a sense of what the main path would have been like at the time. Weddings are even hosted under the walkway. (Courtesy of Jeff Ketterman.)

The pool, once the grand attraction at Rose Island, still remains. This is believed to have been the first filtered swimming pool in the area. The spinning top that was originally in the pool is still in storage. When the park was reopened, the pool actually still held water. Since it was deemed a liability, the pool was drained in 2012 and filled with gravel. (Courtesy of Jeff Ketterman.)

Interpretative panels are found throughout the park. On each, there is also a flood marker indicating the waterline from the 1937 flood. (Courtesy of Jeff Ketterman.)

Panels line the Rose Island trail giving visitors wonderful history and images along the way. When there is no guide available on the walking tour, visitors can take a self-guided visual and audio tour. The park looked into getting electricity, but unfortunately, the cost was going to be an estimated $6 million, as there are no power lines currently near the site. However, the park established the audio tour with the use of a hand crank radio to generate electricity. There are five boxes with four two-minute stories on each. (Courtesy of Jeff Ketterman.)

The interurban trestle crossing Silver Street at the site of Glenwood Park was torn down for a two-lane modern bridge designed for automobiles, and the old track between Jeffersonville and New Albany was no more. (Courtesy of Jeff Ketterman.)

Unfortunately, by 1935, Glenwood Park had become empty and desolate. The property was sold for residential development, and now only the street names give any indication of the great park that was once here. (Courtesy of Jeff Ketterman.)

White City amusement park in Louisville had such a short life that many now do not remember the park. Closed in 1912 and sold for development, no traces of White City remain today. (Courtesy of Jeff Ketterman.)

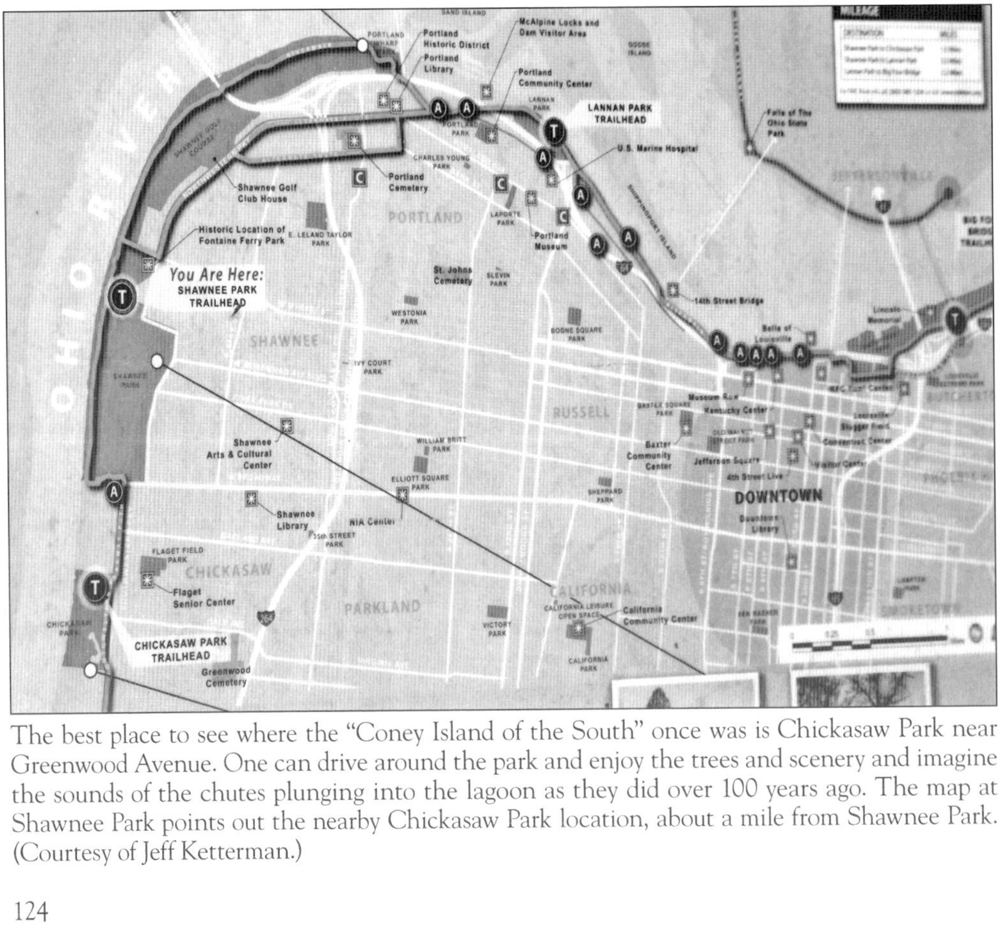

The best place to see where the "Coney Island of the South" once was is Chickasaw Park near Greenwood Avenue. One can drive around the park and enjoy the trees and scenery and imagine the sounds of the chutes plunging into the lagoon as they did over 100 years ago. The map at Shawnee Park points out the nearby Chickasaw Park location, about a mile from Shawnee Park. (Courtesy of Jeff Ketterman.)

Today, the site of Fontaine Ferry is a center for recreation that is part of the Shawnee Park Sports Complex. There are baseball fields and walking trails throughout the park. (Courtesy of Jeff Ketterman.)

Taking a drive on South Western Parkway in West Louisville around Shawnee Park today, one would never know an elaborate amusement park once thrived on the grounds. There are no markers around the property; only a small dot on a park sign points out the general location of Fontaine Ferry Park. This photograph was taken a few years ago and shows the remains of the once great Comet roller coaster. (Courtesy of Johnny Urbanavage.)

Relics of Fontaine Ferry Park can still be found in local antique malls such as Crazy Daisy and Joe Ley's Antiques, as well as from online sellers. Tickets, tokens, banners, and souvenirs are still floating around. (Courtesy of Johnny Urbanavage.)

Souvenirs such as this Fontaine Ferry water cup are now treasures to those who visited the park and remember the fun times they had during the summer, riding the rides and seeing the attractions. (Courtesy of Johnny Urbanavage.)

Today, Kiddieland is just a field. Arlan's Department Store, which was located near Kiddieland and which so many fondly remember, burned down. (Courtesy of Johnny Urbanavage.)

Parts of Kiddieland live on, such as the fire truck, which has been lovingly restored. (Courtesy of Johnny Urbanavage.)